HOW TO READ A COMIC BOOK

Comic books are made up of pictures in boxes, called panels. Look at each of these panels from left to right, and top to bottom.

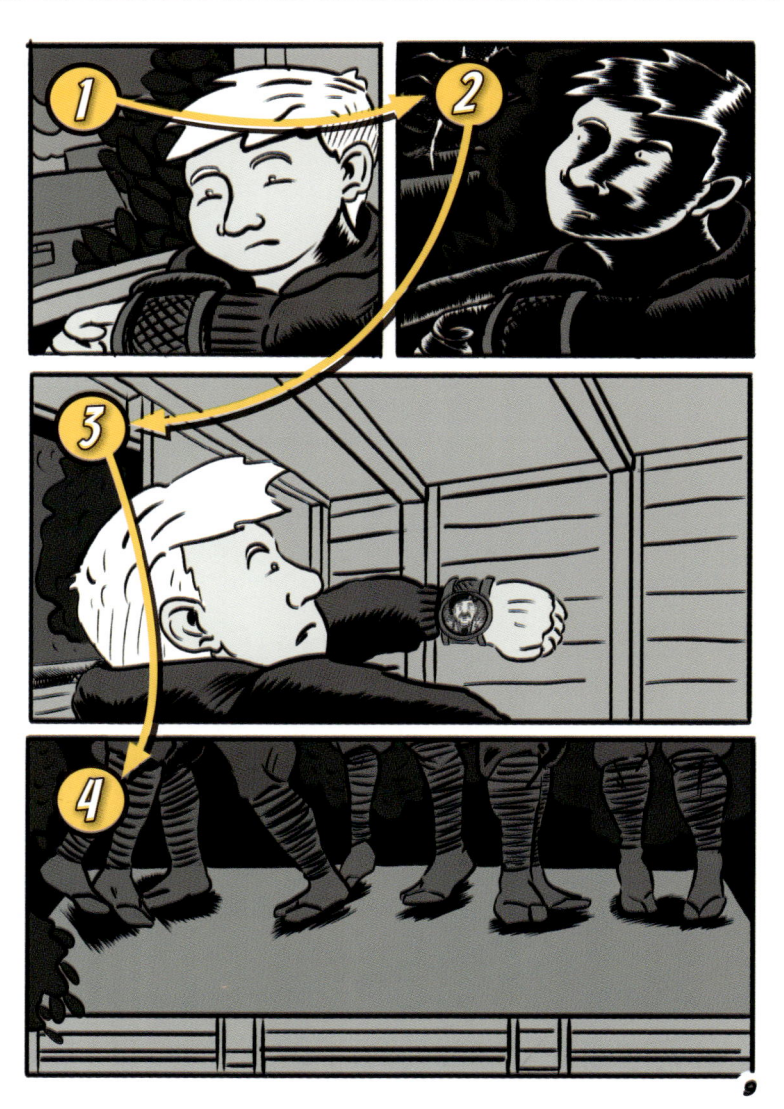

Read the speech bubbles, caption boxes and any sound effects from left to right, too. Together with the images, these will tell you the story.

Bagley might just be the most boring place you have ever seen.

There is nothing special about Bagley at all...

...Nothing except beans.

Lots and lots of beans.

What exactly is going on here, then?

Come down here right now and explain yourselves.

GULP

GULP

She started it!

Did not! Your stupid lumpy bags of beans started this.

@2024 BookLife Publishing Ltd.
King's Lynn, Norfolk, PE30 4LS, UK

ISBN 978-1-80505-283-8

All rights reserved. Printed in India.
A catalogue record for this book is
available from the British Library.

The Beanbag King
Written by Charis Mather
Illustrated by Kris Jones

ABOUT BOOKLIFE GRAPHIC READERS

BookLife Graphic Readers are designed to encourage reluctant readers to take the next step in their reading adventure. These books are a perfect accompaniment to the BookLife Readers phonics scheme and are designed to be read by children who have a good grasp on reading but are reluctant to pick up a full-prose book. Graphic Readers combine graphic and prose storytelling in a way that aids comprehension and presents a more accessible reading experience for reluctant readers and lovers of comic books.

ABOUT THE AUTHOR

I'm Charis! As a young girl, my bedtime stories were made up of 50% epic adventures and 50% dramatic copyright front matter readings. While I can't be completely sure where my inspiration to write books came from, I have my suspicions...

A professional writer at work and a professional daydreamer at home, I spend a lot of time spinning stories in my head, some of which have even made it onto paper!

ABOUT THE ILLUSTRATOR

My name's Kris. If you look very hard you might find me skulking away in my studio somewhere in the ancient land of Wales. It was here that I spent four years at a special drawing school learning to scribble and create nonsense and mayhem on the page for kids to enjoy (and causing a bit of mayhem for my poor teachers, too!)

That was twenty-two years ago. Now, there's nothing I like more than spending my days at home with my wife and my dog, Honey, drawing children's books, cartoons, and comics (with a cup of tea and a biscuit to hand, of course). I do, sometimes, draw serious stuff too – but not very often!

Booklife Readers

The BookLife Readers begin with the very basics of **phonetically decodable reading**. Starting with the earliest step of CVC words – words comprising a consonant, a vowel and a consonant – and building on this combination slowly, the reader follows a prescribed format taken directly from the recognised **Letters and Sounds** educational document.

By aligning our books with Letters and Sounds, we offer our readers a consistent approach to learning, whether at home or in the classroom. Books levelled as 'a' are an introduction to the band. Readers can advance to 'b' where graphemes are consolidated and further graphemes are introduced. The illustrations guide the reader, helping to deliver reading progression through the scheme in a **colourful** and **exciting** way. As a reader moves through the book band levels, the page numbers, level of repetition and sentence structure complexity all advance at a rate which **encourages development** without halting enjoyment.

To find out more about this exciting new reading scheme, visit **www.booklife.co.uk**

BookLife PUBLISHING

BookLife Non-fiction Readers

EXPLORE A WORLD OF NON-FICTION WITH OUR DECODABLE READER RANGE

MORE COMING SOON

Stay Safe Online — 9781839279058
Habitats — 9781839279041

At the Fun Fair — 9781839279010
Look Up! — 9781839279003

At the Shop — 9781839279027
The Fixer's Screws — 9781839279034

Pets — 9781839278976
Picnic — 9781839278969

Vets — 9781839278983
Queens and Kings — 9781839278990

Caterpillar to Butterfly — 9781839278938
Chinese New Year — 9781839278921

Dig a Pit — 9781839278945
Tap the Puck — 9781839278952

Which of these steps comes first?

About Reading

When we read a book, we go from left to right, like this:

Some books just have pictures, like this:

Some books have words and pictures, like this:

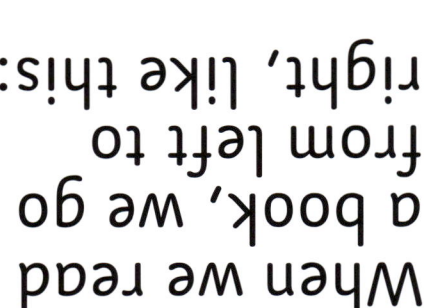

©2021 **BookLife Publishing Ltd.**
King's Lynn, Norfolk PE30 4LS

ISBN 978-1-83927-893-8

All rights reserved. Printed in England.
A catalogue record for this book is available
from the British Library.

Caterpillar to Butterfly
Written by William Anthony
Designed by Jasmine Pointer

An Introduction to BookLife Readers...

Our Readers have been specifically created in line with the London Institute of Education's approach to book banding and are phonetically decodable and ordered to support each phase of Letters and Sounds.

Each book has been created to provide the best possible reading and learning experience. Our aim is to share our love of books with children, providing both emerging readers and prolific page-turners with beautiful books that are guaranteed to provoke interest and learning, regardless of ability.

BOOK BAND GRADED using the Institute of Education's approach to levelling.

PHONETICALLY DECODABLE supporting each phase of Letters and Sounds.

EXERCISES AND QUESTIONS to offer reinforcement and to ascertain comprehension.

CLEAR DESIGN to inspire and provoke engagement, providing the reader with clear visual representations of each non-fiction topic.

AUTHOR INSIGHT:
WILLIAM ANTHONY

Despite his young age, William Anthony's involvement with children's education is quite extensive. He has written over 60 titles with BookLife Publishing so far, across a wide range of subjects. William graduated from Cardiff University with a 1st Class BA (Hons) in Journalism, Media and Culture, creating an app and a TV series, among other things, during his time there.

William Anthony has also produced work for the Prince's Trust, a charity created by HRH The Prince of Wales, that helps young people with their professional future. He has created animated videos for a children's education company that works closely with the charity.

This book focuses on inspiring imagination and interest. This is a lilac level 0 book band.

Image Credits: Images are courtesy of Shutterstock.com. With thanks to Getty Images, Thinkstock Photo and iStockphoto. Front Cover – Kim Pin, andregric. p4–5 – Sarah2, Kumbaya Photography. p6–7 – Marsha Mood. p8–9 – Liz Weber. p10–11 – ChameleonsEye, dossyl. p12 – Liz Weber. p17 – Visanuwit thongon.

Caterpillar to Butterfly

Level 0 – Lilac